FROM ILFORD TO HAINAULT

Barkingside tram at the Broadway. Ilford has always been a significant crossroads and the Great Essex Road, originally laid down by the Romans, ran east to west, although earlier trackways had preceded it. South of the crossroads lay an important route from near the leper hospital to the great Abbey of Barking, founded by the Saxons. North, beyond the tram, was once a lane that led into the forest. After 1903 a municipal tramway service operated from here to the Horns district of Barkingside.

FROM ILFORD TO HAINAULT

*Featuring Barkingside, Fairlop, Woodford Green, Woodford Bridge,
Hainault Forest, Chigwell*

DON HEWSON

SUTTON PUBLISHING LIMITED

Sutton Publishing Limited
Phoenix Mill · Thrupp · Stroud
Gloucestershire · GL5 2BU

First published 1996

Copyright © Don Hewson, 1996

British Library Cataloguing in Publication Data
A catalogue record for this book is available from the
British Library.

ISBN 0-7509-1008-9

Typeset in 10/12 Perpetua.
Typesetting and origination by
Sutton Publishing Limited.
Printed in Great Britain by
Ebenezer Baylis, Worcester.

The hospital carnival in Cranbrook Road, 1907. It drew crowds from a wide area, offering the most spectacular shows, ingenious floats and costumes which were worked on throughout the year in spare moments.

CONTENTS

The clock tower at the centre of the Broadway, seen here in 1906, was once Ilford's best known feature. It formed an informal grandstand for the idler to watch the passing scene from 1901 until it was removed as an obstruction to tram traffic in 1903 and rebuilt in South Park. It was destroyed by a flying bomb during the Second World War.

INTRODUCTION

The ancient remains of mammoth, rhinoceros, elephant, hippopotamus, wild horse, elk, stag, bison, bear, wolf, fox, lion and water-rat have been discovered in the area covered by this book. Sometime in the remote past prehistoric man also discovered the advantages of this district near the Thames and on the banks of the Roding. These traces of early inhabitants have often been found in brick-earth pits which were worked in the nineteenth and early twentieth centuries to provide homes for modern man. At Uphall Camp near the Roding and the Barking boundary, pottery from a Middle Iron Age settlement of the second century BC has been unearthed; nearby excavation revealed round-houses, including some with porches, and agricultural storage shelters of similar construction. These discoveries suggest that a successful community flourished here at that time. During the years of forest living (from medieval times to the eighteenth century), when the forest of Essex stretched down to Ilford and to the Great Essex Road, built by the Romans, the local charcoal burners retained the skill and custom of building very similar huts. An illustration of one constructed during a brief revival of charcoal burning at the beginning of the twentieth century appears in this book (see p. 100).

The name 'Ilford' dates from pre-Norman times when small communities along the River Roding each called their own stretch of water, which passed through their jealously-guarded territory, by different names. At Ilford they called it 'the Hile', meaning 'the trickling stream', from which 'Il' was derived. It eventually became Ilford, 'the ford through the trickling stream'. Hainault comes from 'higna holt', meaning the monastic community wood. The wood belonged to the ancient abbey of Barking, as did much of Ilford during the Middle Ages.

Ilford owes its existence to the foundation of this abbey by St Ethelwald, who created it for his sister. The abbey at first housed both monks and nuns. Ilford was at the junction where the route to the abbey's isolated marshland site diverted from the main road between London and Essex. The influence of the abbey was felt when a lazar house or leper hospital was founded by the abbess during the reign of King Stephen. Provision was made for thirteen lepers, a prior, a master and other staff. The hospital chapel stands in the same spot to this day. The Roman road, neglected to a large extent in the Dark Ages, was well-used again as medieval commerce and trade grew. Other links were also established between London and Essex. Travellers, rich and poor, journeyed along these roads on horse or foot and risked ambush or robbery in some lonely spot. Over the centuries there were rich pickings for outlaws, footpads, robbers and highwaymen, such as Dick Turpin. Once they had committed their crime they could melt back into the woodland to the north or thickets and marshland to the south. Royal connections at Havering Palace and Hornchurch, the capital of the Royal Liberty of Havering further to the east, brought great processions out from London. The royal personages were protected by huge retinues of soldiers, courtiers and attendants.

Ilford was visited by many kings and queens, foreign royalty, ambassadors, writers and continental travellers who passed through on their way to and from the ports at Tilbury and Harwich. However, it was not until the nineteenth century that the hamlet began to acquire more important trappings such as a separate ecclesiastical parish and church, a railway and stations, and finally, with the breaking up and selling off of the old farming estates, an ever increasing tide of houses and suddenly a huge population. Ilford was ready to break away from its mother town of centuries past – it was no longer a part of Barking. It rapidly acquired its own civic pride and municipal institutions, tramways, an electricity undertaking, a fine town hall and eventually the best transport links of any London suburb.

Ilford's impressive communication network was a continuing factor in its incredible growth. The arrival of the railway did not at first make the impact it should have done. The early Eastern Counties Railway was rather inefficient in attracting customers. It was burdened with debt during most of its history and unable to promote its services effectively. Like many other railways in the mid-nineteenth century it saw special cheap excursions from London to the coast as a means of making a profit. The commuter traffic was negligible. As the old farming estates near the centre of Ilford began to be sold off for development, this situation slowly began to change. The Great Eastern Railway took over the main line through Ilford from most of the smaller rail Companies in East Anglia in 1862. It was soon in dire financial straits. But it recovered and was soon co-operating with local developers to improve travel by rail from Ilford. William Pallant, the station-master, saw a transformation – a wayside village halt grew into a frantically busy suburban station with its own terminus platform. The new station opened in July 1894 and put Ilford firmly on the commuter map. By 1900 this expansion had seen two lines increase to five; 90 daily trains to 500; 7 staff to 200. One of Ilford's main developers, A. Cameron Corbett MP, paid for a separate exit and entrance to his Grange Estate, north of the line. As each new estate was constructed, improvements in rail travel were made. The growth of the estates and the expansion of the rail network soon made Ilford into one of London's main commuter suburbs. Tram and then bus services to the north, west and east created more suburbs. However, these services became less significant with the rise in car-ownership and after the extension of the Central Line underground railway to Gants Hill, Newbury Park and the old stations on the Hainault loop line opened at the end of the Second World War.

THE STREETS OF ILFORD

A very large crowd at Ilford Broadway celebrate the 1906 carnival in style. The High Road entrance eastwards is at the top left-hand side. This view is taken from the clock tower.

Ilford Post Office decorated for George V's Silver Jubilee in 1935. There had been a postal receiving house at Ilford in the 1790s and in the same decade there was a Penny Post service in the local district .

The sign of the sweep (note the brush above window) possibly on Ilford Hill in August 1927. The sweep's trade was still important in the days of coal fires and his cart was to be seen everywhere.

A view of the street by the hospital chapel on Ilford Hill, 1923. All the traffic is pedestrian — people still mostly walked to the shops and even to their place of work if it was local.

Breton onion-sellers in Ilford, August 1927. Before the days of supermarkets these men came annually from France to hawk their wares around the streets.

Poulter's milk float in the old hand-pushed style, with ladles and jugs, 1927.

Horse-drawn milk float, Cranbrook Road, August 1927.

J.F. Wenden's coal lorry filling up with sacks at the High Road Railway Coal Depot, late 1920s.

Ilford Town Hall exterior with passers-by, 1907. This was erected on part of the former Clements farmland estate in 1901. It was later extended to include a public library on the Oakfield Road side and further enlarged in 1933.

The council chamber at the town hall, 1906. Note the overhead fan to cope with hot Edwardian summers or cool the hot air created during debates!

The fine public hall built as part of the town hall. The new Ilford Council, formed in 1888 after the area was removed from the control of Barking, was extremely progressive. Within a decade between 1891 and 1901 projects for improved sewerage, baths, an isolation hospital, a fire station, several parks and an electricity and tramway scheme were developed.

The town hall surrounded by shops in the High Road, 1920. The new council first met above shops in Cranbrook Road and then from 1898 in a schoolroom at Ilford Hall in the High Road.

A view of the excellent shopping centre already in existence by the 1920s. A horse-drawn coal cart is visible in the near distance and two men are working in the middle of the road by a removed manhole cover. It was safe to leave your bike at the kerb unchained at this time.

A view of the Broadway from Ilford Lane, 1925. A route no. 25 or 26 bus and an Ilford tram are seen with the White Horse pub to the right of the centre. The Ilford Hippodrome is on the far right.

A tram from Loxford Bridge turns towards Chadwell Heath in the centre of the Broadway, 1905.

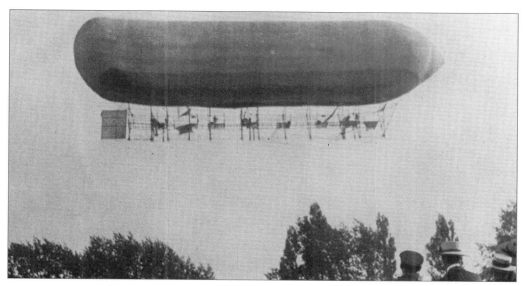

The Barton-Rawson airship lifting off, Saturday 22 July 1905. It made a flight from the Alexandra Palace, circling Ilford twice, and then heading towards Barkingside.

The R101 photographed above Ilford in 1930. The massive diesel powered airship was 722 ft long. It crashed in flames on its proving flight in the same year.

Station Approach, Ilford, 1920s. Commuters and shoppers take on the traffic as they spill across the road. Three older men on the right-hand pavement are the only ones with time to stand and watch the photographer. A few pedestrians are moving too fast for the camera film speed to capture them.

Albert Gibson Wilson's newsagent's and stationer's shop at 96 High Road, 1912. A plethora of signs and displays divert the attention. The once familiar 'eye' sign denotes an optician's (T.L. Wilson) upstairs. Another sign on the wall, with a bell symbol, denotes the availability of a public telephone in the shop.

A class of girls at Christchurch Road School, 1906. This school, situated in Wellesley Road, was opened in 1900.

The not very busy High Road shopping area near Moulton's, the department store, in the 1950s. In 1959 Moulton's was badly damaged by the fire which destroyed Harrison Gibson's, also a department store.

'God and Mammon'. The juxtaposition of the High Road Catholic Church with a film poster and a shop selling bathroom fittings was distasteful to many people at this time.

A most enthusiastic men's meeting at the Congregational church, *c.* 1905. These were great days for this church under its charismatic leader, Henry Vine, and this church was later renamed the Vine Memorial Church after his death.

Ilford vicarage, 1912. Clergymen were extremely well respected and through the many church groups and societies that existed they were able to make a great impact on the social and spiritual welfare of the residents of Ilford's new estates.

AWAY FROM IT ALL

The joys of the open air – an allotment at Clay Hall. Many of the newcomers to the Ilford area were able to grow their own produce to help the family budget. The allotment gardens or smallholdings also had the merit of keeping a man out of his wife's way in their often not very spacious new home. The neat hut seen here was obviously an enjoyable retreat.

The pleasures of flying – actually a bicycle decorated by F.M. Connellan for a carnival.

Approach to the Old King's Head, Chigwell, 1909. There were excellent bicycle rides to picturesque spots all round Ilford. Chigwell was an easy destination for a half-day holiday.

Chigwell in 1909. Time off was precious and most homes in Edwardian Ilford had several bicycles to provide exercise and recreational outings to nearby beauty spots.

Woodford Bridge, 1929. This was a local beauty spot.

Around Ilford in 1908 there were refreshment houses like this one to serve the needs of cyclists and trippers. These were found at places such as Aldborough Hatch, Fairlop, Little Heath and Hainault.

AN . .

OPEN

PING-PONG

Under the . .
Rules of . .
the Ping-Pong
Association. .

TOURNAMENT

Will be held in Marquee.

Committee :

Dr. T. B. JOBSON, *Chairman.*

Mrs. LACH-SZYRMA.	Miss TROLOVE.
Mrs. APPLEYARD.	Mr. R. HILL.
Miss GREEN.	Mr. H. HILL.
Miss BEST.	Mr. W. TROLOVE.
Miss HILL.	Dr. W. APPLEYARD.

Admission to Tent :
SIXPENCE
Each Person.

Mr. H. HARRIS, *Hon. Treasurer.*

Mr. W. N. HILLS, *Hon. Secretary.*

The Prizes will be distributed to the Successful Competitors on THURSDAY Evening

By Mrs. HERBERT INGLEBY.

Details from a ping-pong tournament programme and souvenir of a bazaar and garden party at Valentine's, 28/29 May 1902. The hostess, Mrs Ingleby, lady of the manor at Valentine's, was a great fundraiser – in this case the aim was to build a house for the clergy in the Beehive district of Ilford.

At the wishing well, Valentine's Park, 1920s. This lady is wearing fashionable clothes of the time.

Locals skating on the frozen lake at Valentine's, January 1917. The park was gradually created as Mrs Ingleby, the owner of Valentine's Estate, donated land to the town of Ilford over the years. The lake area was one of the first parts made available to local people, who made the most of it all through the year.

Hardy swimmers of Valentine's Swimming Club about to plunge into the lake for a 60 yards handicap race, Christmas morning, 1919. The lake had frozen over at Christmas time two years before.

These swimmers, left to right, finished first, second and third respectively. Swimming in Valentine's Lake was popular as it was so close to the centre of town and as a sport it did not require costly equipment. Valentine's Park was at first called Central Park or Cranbrook Park. As it expanded and took over farmland the name changed.

YE FUNNIE MANNE OF YE VALENTINES
SWIMMINGE CLUBBE ON YE CHRISTMASSE
MORNE IN YE YEAR 1919

An example of the amusement that locals devised for themselves before the age of television. Photography was considered a novelty and in every organization there were keen amateur photographers and somebody was always ready to pose for the camera.

The saloon bar of the Angel Hotel, 1906; this was a male recreational preserve.

Ilford Football Club seen in a line-up at the beginning of the twentieth century, possibly with the Essex Senior Cup. The club was founded in 1881.

Ilford Football Club on their Barcelona Tour, 1922; a very debonair group. It was becoming popular for Essex teams to tour the continent at this time.

The ladies have crept into this group representing Ilford Cricket Club at the 1906 carnival.

ILFORD. BROAD WAY.

Ilford Broadway, with the Ilford Hippodrome on the right, in the late 1930s. The hippodrome, which was opened in 1909, was a very popular place of entertainment. It cost £35,000 to construct at the height of the music hall and variety theatre boom. There was room for 2,500 patrons to be seated and for 500 to stand at each performance, usually twice nightly with matinées on certain days. On 12 January 1945 the curtain had just risen on the pantomime *Robinson Crusoe* when a German V2 rocket dived into some cottages behind, killing fifteen people and gutting the theatre. It was finally demolished in 1957 after decaying stone on the frontage fell on a passing bus.

In the High Road, south side, beyond the Broadway was the De Luxe Cinema, opened in 1911. The cinema was just the other side of A.G. Wilson's shop seen on pages 22 and 23.

The Super Cinema on the right with its café lounge opened to a warm reception in 1922. Britons were becoming star struck with the Hollywood movies and the centre of Ilford was now quite an entertainment complex for a wide locality. A C & A shop now occupies this area.

The Savoy, a more recent cinema, later to become the Odeon, opened at Gants Hill, late 1940s. After the Second World War, as with the end of the First World War, there were large audiences wishing to indulge in the escapism of glamorous films after the horrors of wartime. Queues like this one were not uncommon, snaking all round the outside of the building. Television was not yet commonplace in most homes in the late 1940s and early 1950s.

NORTH VIA CRANBROOK ROAD

The Wash, Cranbrook Road, a charming spot where the stream crossed the road from Valentine's Park (previously known as Central Park and Cranbrook Park) which can be seen in the background to the right. In the days of horse-drawn carts, horse and rider would be driven into the water to cool off. Eventually redevelopment took place and the wash was removed, a telephone exchange being built on the site.

Garden City from Cranbrook Road, 1912. These delightful roads were created in a separate, small area between Cranbrook Road and the Valentine's Estate, later part of Valentine's Park. They had nearby access to an open space as well as being close to a shopping centre, buses and a railway station. Note that no cars are visible in this scene. The Garden City was a slightly scaled down version of the innovative garden suburbs elsewhere, where the houses were often individually designed.

Near the bottom of Cranbrook Road, 1904. York Road opens to the right by 'Bank' corner. Until recently the right-hand side of the road nearest the camera had been occupied by the gardens of a house behind a high wall. The large, overhanging lamps outside the shops on the left were designed to illuminate the interior of the shops as well. Lights inside shops were rare at this time due to the risk of fire.

Cranbrook College, 1929. This was one of
several schools and colleges on nearby
Cranbrook Road at this time.

Cranbrook school sports day, 1930.

A group photograph of the girls and younger boys of Clark's College, 1930s. Originally Clark's School for Boys was founded in 1880, and at its height it had twenty-eight branches all around London. Clark's School at Ilford began in 1915 and developed separate units for boys and girls; it closed in 1974. Part of the old boys' school became an army recruiting office.

Ursuline High School, 1924. This school was founded in 1903 and is listed in the 1908 Kelly's Directory at 71 and 79 Cranbrook Road. The principal was Madame Mary Bowen.

St Clement's Church, Park Avenue, viewed from the park, 1916. In 1908 the clergy here consisted of no fewer than six – a vicar and five curates who ministered to the needs of the fast growing population of the Cranbrook area. Flats (35–63 Park Avenue) now stand on this site.

Wycliffe Congregational Church, erected in 1907, is situated in the part of Cranbrook Road before The Drive. It was originally Christ Church before amalgamating with another congregation, superseding the original iron church. In more recent times it became the Ilford Playhouse, home of local drama groups.

The Lodge at the beginning of the entrance drive to Cranbrook Hall, 1929, long after The Drive had become a residential road. Further development on what was known as the Cranbrook Castle Estate took place in the mid-1920s, the houses being sold by the Griggs estate agency in 1926. Cranbrook Hall was demolished in 1900 and Cranbrook Castle in 1923. The Cranbrook Estate was begun in 1897. This followed the completion of the Grange Estate in 1894 in the area closest to Ilford station. Before the First World War buses served these estates via Cranbrook Road and services expanded to the north as new estates were built.

The Drive and Lodge in 1905.

This view from the 1920s includes from left to right, The Lodge and entrance to The Drive, Russell Daniels's nursery garden building, the wash pond and a General Company bus serving the Cranbrook Road.

This building on The Drive was typical of the substantial houses erected in this area. It is seen here in 1920.

Cranbrook Castle is seen in the distance beyond the peaceful River Roding. The castle was built as a mausoleum, but was never used as such.

The Roding in full flood at Wanstead Park during 1903. Such floods not only swamped the meadows but also the housing estates built close to the river.

The result of a flooded Roding is this waterlogged scene in Empress Avenue, 1903. Builders of these houses had not considered the possible impact of new drainage flows and storm surges along the Roding. Although the flood was enjoyed by chidren and journalists, local householders, who had to mop up, and insurers, who had to pay out, were not so amused.

Gants Hill, 1950s. Cranbrook Road once continued without interruption between hedges to the north. When Eastern Avenue was built in the mid-1920s the area at the junction gradually took on urban aspects with shops, offices, banks, a cinema and finally, after the Second World War, a tube station on the Central Line extension. In its early years Eastern Avenue was a peaceful backwater with little traffic except at weekends and holidays, when everyone with a car made the journey to Southend. There are stories of children learning to ride bikes and rollerskate along its wide open spaces at quiet times. During the Second World War tunnels constructed for the new Central Line had a different use – until after the war, they housed a linear factory run by Plesseys to produce goods for the war effort.

A HELPING HAND

The Lord Mayor laying the foundation stone of Ilford's new hospital, April 1910. To be known as the Ilford Emergency Hospital, Abbey Road, Newbury Park, it was opened for use in 1912.

Dressing up for a special day, 1910. In order to raise money for the proposed Ilford Hospital an annual carnival was held throughout the Edwardian era until the First World War.

Entrants in the carnival were not shy of making themselves look ridiculous as it was all in a good cause, 1916.

Floats such as this one with an Indian Durbar theme were often quite magnificent in concept and execution.

Children in fancy dress wait to be judged – note the young lady holding a placard with a contemporary suffragette message.

Loxford Ward's dairy float. There was strong competition for prizes between the different wards into which the new municipal Ilford was divided.

Ilford Sanatorium. The innovative regime of light and air was introduced into new hospital units to aid the recovery of victims of tuberculosis – then a great scourge among young and old.

The Ilford Emergency Hospital, 1920s, was built with verandas to help its patients' convalescence on sunny days.

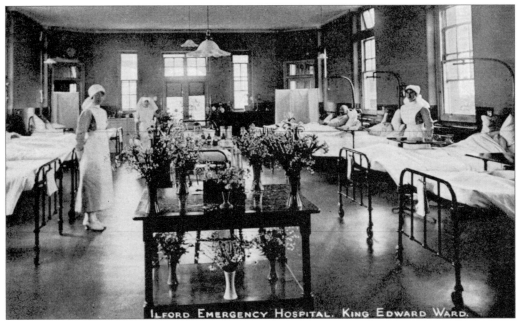

A view inside the King Edward Ward showing the strict regime of cleanliness and order then prevalent, 1920s.

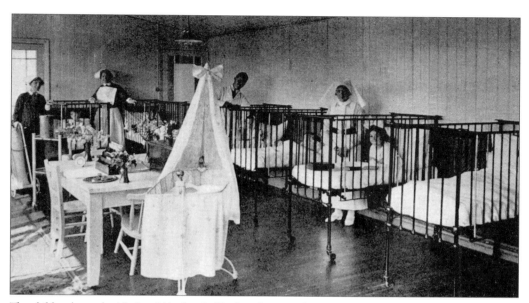

The children's ward with the old high-sided beds and a special nursery cot by sister's table, 1920s.

A view of the Ilford Emergency Hospital during the First World War. The hospital had to cope with an influx of wounded and sick soldiers from France and Belgium at this time.

King George V Hospital, late 1930s. This was a rebuilding of the original emergency hospital on more or less the same site with funds raised in Ilford and Barking. The original hospital was on a rather out-of-the-way site. The construction of the arterial road in the mid-1920s made it more accessible. Health was becoming a more important issue and there were now insurance and hospital saving schemes which the skilled artisan and more successful workman could afford. The construction of hospitals like the one seen here improved the standard of local hospital care. Many London-based specialists attended cases in the suburban hospitals with their often more up-to-date facilities.

KING   GEORGE   HOSPITAL

Figures Speak Louder than Words

SEVEN YEARS GROWTH

1927		1934	
In-Patients	- 828	In-Patients	**3,242**
Out-Patient attendances	- 6,250	Out-Patient attendances	**104,361**

£40,000 | **£18,950**

per annum required
for Maintenance | required to Liquidate
Building Fund Debt

DO YOU SUBSCRIBE?

DOES THIS WORK DESERVE REFUSAL?

Contributions and offers of personal service will be gratefully acknowledged by
the Secretary and Superintendent.

The new hospital was still heavily dependent on
subscriptions and contributions.

The justices of the county of Middlesex bought Claybury in 1887 in order to establish a lunatic asylum in
the peace of the countryside. It was hoped this would assist the recovery of the insane. The new London
County Council acquired the asylum and completed it in 1893.

Dr Barnardo at work in his office, *c.* 1903. As soon as he was qualified, Barnardo took up the challenge to provide a safe haven for London's orphan and destitute children.

The famous depiction of Barnardo as 'Father of Nobody's Children'. He literally worked himself into an early grave for this cause. Every penny was spent in the cause leaving little for office administration, which Barnardo almost single-handedly took on his own shoulders.

A 'family' group of girls outside Mayflower Cottage at the Dr Barnardo Girls' Home in Barkingside.

The study and library at the Girls' Model Village (a Dr Barnardo home), Barkingside. The unusual name of this children's home was derived from the fact that the homes in Barkingside formed a village with its own hospital, chapel and teaching facilities.

This aerial view shows the generous lay out of the Dr Barnardo Girls' Home and its rural surroundings in the 1920s.

Residents taking the air in the grounds of the Model Village.

Sanatorium patients catch the sun.

The end of the first chapter of the Barnardo story, 1905. The funeral procession with Barnardo's coffin preceded by the clergy leaves the conveniently placed Barkingside station.

Ilford Urban District Council's Ley Street Fire Station built in 1905 with its new motorized fire engines ready for action in the 1920s. This new fire station superseded the one in Oakfield Road built in 1893.

There were also substations at Horns Road and Cranbrook Road. The first motorized engines were introduced in 1914.

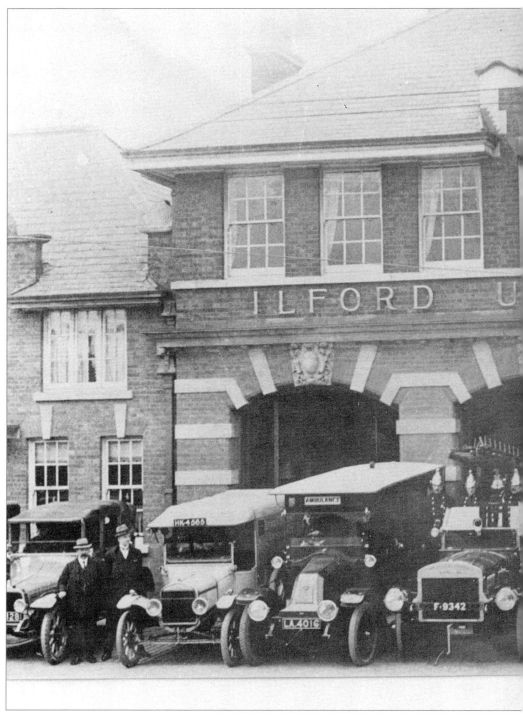

A fine line-up of the borough's emergency vehicles outside the fire station in the late 1920s. Ilford was a progressive authority as can be seen from the range of vehicles in the photograph. It was unusual to have all the emergency vehicles in a single location.

In less picturesque uniform, but ready for all eventualities, are members of an Ilford Auxiliary Fire Service team during the Second World War.

A smart lady driver stands by her vehicle at an Ilford Ambulance Station during the Second World War. Women proved their worth as drivers of emergency vehicles in many Essex towns.

YESTERDAY'S BARKINGSIDE

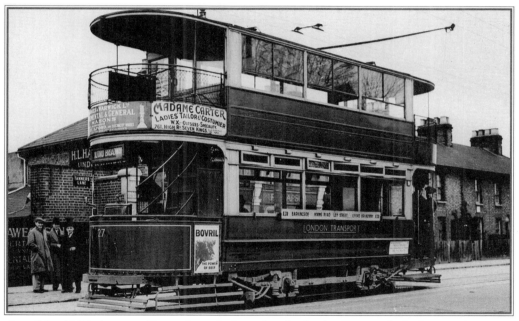

One of the old Ilford trams at Tanners Lane, Barkingside, after London Transport had taken over the service.

You can lead a horse to water – Lambs Farm, Barkingside, August 1904. The joys of a country walk from
the tram terminus at the beginning of the century are well illustrated by this country scene. Dozens of
footpaths stretched across the farmland now occupied by the pavement, houses and roads of Ilford's
suburbs. In Edwardian times George Tasker published a booklet of walks in this area of the countryside.
One of the walks started at Ilford station and continued along Cranbrook road to the countryside. This
was before the construction of Eastern Avenue. The London General Bus Company also produced leaflets
detailing walks from their termini, especially in the Hainault Forest area. However, the bus routes
themselves encouraged commuters to move to the area and soon after the end of the First World War
many old footpaths were buried under new housing estates.

Barkingside, 1905. Although the terminus of a tram route, it was still quite an old-fashioned village.

In 1906 Horns Road had a rural aspect despite the tram line poles.

Fern Hall, Roding Lane, September 1928. This was one of Ilford's neat country houses of the sort favoured at one time by rich London merchants. Some of these rural retreats are shown on the Chapman and Andre map of 1777. During the nineteenth century the larger estates were broken down into smaller units and during the Victorian period many new houses were built on the forest fringe. The forest was being reduced even before the deforestation of the 1850s – this was by order of Parliament and created more agricultural land by destroying large areas of woodland.

The wheelwright at Barkingside in the 1920s. There was still a trade in shoeing horses, some repairs to carts and even work on the new-fangled motor car. Such picturesque scenes as these were fast disappearing. The rise of the motor vehicle and motorization of farm vehicles and implements eventually made it impossible for these craftsmen to earn a living without converting their business into garages and service stations.

Entrance to Dunsprings Farm, 1924. In the middle of the nineteenth century the farm consisted of 75 acres and was leased separately as part of the Monins' family estate up to 1918. Today such farms as these have been replaced by streets and horses and this way of life, which existed in Ilford for many centuries, has disappeared.

A view of Redbridge House from Roding Lane, September 1928.

Gaysham Hall, 1929. One of the most intriguing old buildings in the area to modern local historians.

Gaysham Hall viewed from the north, September 1927. In the 1920s the current house was described as having been built of brick early in the seventeenth century with a wing added on the south-east side in the eighteenth century. The name dates back to Roger de Gaysham who lived here in the late thirteenth century. Thomas de Sandwich owned Gaysham Hall at one time. He was victualler to the

Black Prince (Edward, Prince of Wales) and died in 1360. In May 1361 Gaysham, along with other properties passed to the Prince of Wales as security for debts owed to him by Sandwich. In early medieval times Gaysham Hall was a free tenement held by Barking until about 1400 when it became part of the abbey's demesne.

The dining room at Gaysham Hall showing the fireplace and panelling, 9 September 1927. The original ancient Gaysham manor was said to be 'of timber and very spacious'; it was supposedly pulled down by Henry Wight, who died in 1716. However, this photograph shows a room which probably preserves part

of the original construction. It is more likely that the original building was merely extended and altered. The house was seriously damaged by a flying bomb in 1944, leading to its demolition in 1947.

Corner of North Room on the upper floor
of Gaysham Hall, 9 September 1927.

Seymour Gardens, 1914.

A view of old Mossford Green, 1929. A view that could have come from any of the rural counties of England.

Gaysham Hall Farm, 1929.

High Street, Barkingside, mid-1930s. A housebuilder's exhibition has been erected on the vacant site on the left. Gradually the new shopping parades are rising along the road – the gardens of a new development can be seen in the distance.

Tram at Tanners Lane, Barkingside, January 1938. There seem to be more staff than passengers aboard this tram. The three young boys on the left are enjoying a gossip outside H.L. Hawes, the undertaker's.

The newly rebuilt Chequers public house, 1930s. Several buildings of the same name previously stood on this site. The new Chequers pub was prepared for the increased business created by the housing estates.

Haigville Gardens, Barkingside; one of the new streets of houses.

Brinkworth Road rises from the fields.

HAINAULT AND FAIRLOP

This hiker striding along into Hainault Forest in the 1920s has probably alighted from one of the buses in the distance. The General Bus Company put out a leaflet describing the countryside and walks around Hainault with details of the new bus services operating in the forest area.

Looking through Hainault Forest to an open glade, *c.* 1910. This is a characteristic view of the forest which, in medieval times, was developed to include clearings where the wild animals could be driven out into the open where they could be watched by royal spectators in grandstands among the trees.

A Hainault clearing, 1913.

A wayside seat, 1913. One of a series of artistic photographs of the picturesque beauty spots of Hainault
Forest in imitation of earlier Victorian landscape paintings. In many ways the fringes of the forest
remained rural. Many of the small cottages and shacks did not have proper lighting, heating or sanitation;
and this situation continued into the 1920s and '30s. Local people still walked to Romford market and
back in a day at this time.

The keeper's lodge – Hog Hill House, 1851. This building was situated on a high point with good views of the changing forest landscape.

The Beehive Hotel, 1906. This was a favourite place for walkers and riders in the forest to stop for refreshment.

A side view of Hainault Lodge, 1913. It can be seen marked on the map of the forest (1908) reproduced on page 98. This lodge was once a large private house situated in an isolated spot on the edge of Hainault Forest. The house still exists and has had a variety of uses.

The Hainault Forest bus to and from Grange Hill station waiting at the Beehive Hotel. Visitors to the forest to see relatives or merely for pleasure were able to reach otherwise inaccessible areas by travelling on this bus. The Beehive was one of numerous refreshment centres available to the summertime tourist.

In the winter the hotel was mostly only frequented by locals. The Fairlop loop railway line to and from Ilford began operating in 1903 and opened up the whole forest area in the days before cars were commonplace.

Dido was one of the characters of the forest who came to Chigwell Row in the summer of 1880. He was well known for his knowledge and application of herbal remedies, effecting many amazing cures for local people. He lived a gypsy-like existence but was not born a gypsy. After his death it transpired that his name was William Bell and he had at one time been a docker. It was thought that he came to the forest and chose his name because he had been thwarted in love, as the mythical character of Dido, from Virgil's *Aeneid*, had been.

A gypsy encampment in the forest.

A gypsy caravan on the fringe of the forest. When Hainault Forest was deforested in the mid-nineteenth century and much of it turned into agricultural land, the gypsies lost their old haunts. They were forced to linger on the outskirts of communities and camp, for instance, along the river banks in places like Collier Row and Marks Gate. In time a community with gypsy characteristics grew up here. They stood out from the other inhabitants though there were some intermarriages. Many made money by selling home-made items, such as pegs, around the nearby suburbs. They also visited Romford market where many gypsies traded in horses. From time to time gypsies from all over the country would visit this area. Many non-gypsies were attracted to this way of life and eked out a living in the Hainault area; Dido was one example (see opposite page).

Here the tight lass, knives, combs, and scissors spies,
And *looks* on thimbles with desiring eyes.
The mountebank now treads the stage, and sells
His pills, his balsams, and his ague-spells:
Now o'er and o'er the nimble tumbler springs,
And on the rope the vent'rous maiden swings;
Jack Pudding, in his party-coloured jacket,
Tosses the glove, and jokes at ev'ry packet:
Here raree-shows are seen, and Punch's feats,
And pockets picked in crowds and various cheats.

Mr Day had thus the satisfaction of introducing the appearances of civilisation in a district which had heretofore been chiefly noted as a haunt of banditti.

Fun of this kind, like fame, naturally gathers force as it goes along. We learn that for some years before the death of Mr Day, which took place in 1767, the pump-and-block-makers of Wapping, to the amount of thirty or forty, used to come each first Friday of July to the Fairlop beans-and-bacon feast, seated in a boat formed of a single piece of wood, and mounted upon wheels, covered with an awning, and drawn by six horses. As they went accompanied by a band of musicians,

FAIRLOP OAK.

it may be readily supposed how the country-people would flock round, attend, and stare at their anomalous vehicle, as it hurled madly along the way to the forest. A local poet, who had been one of the company, gives us just a faint hint of the feelings connected with this journey:

'O'er land our vessel bent its course,
Guarded by troops of foot and horse;
Our anchors they were all a-peak,
Our crew were baling from each leak,
On Stratford bridge it made me quiver,
Lest they should spill us in the river.'

The founder of the Fairlop Festival was remarkable for benevolence and a few innocent eccentricities. He was never married, but bestowed as much kindness upon the children of a sister as he could have spent upon his own. He had a female servant, a widow, who had been eight-and-twenty years with him. As she had in life loved two things in especial, her wedding-ring and her tea, he caused her to be buried with the former on her finger, and a pound of tea in each hand—the latter

circumstance being the more remarkable, as he himself disliked tea, and made no use of it. He had a number of little aversions, but no resentments. It changed the usual composed and amiable expression of his countenance to hear of any one going to law. He literally every day relieved the poor at his gate. He often lent sums of money to deserving persons, charging no interest for it. When he had attained a considerable age, the Fairlop Oak lost one of its branches. Accepting the fact as an omen of his own approaching end, he caused the detached limb of the tree to be fashioned into a coffin for himself, and this convenience he took care to *try*, lest it should prove too short. By his request, his body was borne in its coffin to Barking churchyard by water, in a boat, the worthy old gentleman having contracted a prejudice against all land vehicles, the living horse included, in consequence of being so often thrown from them in his various journeys.*

* *Fairlop and its Founder*, printed at Totham, 1847.

22

The Fairlop Oak (from the *Book of Days*). This was a meeting place for gypsies since the early days of the Fairlop Fair. They travelled from all parts of Britain to this reunion place. After the deforestation of 1851 the land where the great oak had stood was enclosed. The annual meeting place was transferred to land near the Bald-Faced Hind public house.

A new Fairlop Oak public house replaced the old one and is seen here in the 1930s.

A souvenir of the inauguration of Fairlop Playing Fields, 22 May 1909. The popularity of the Fairlop area as a public resort for leisure and recreation continued.

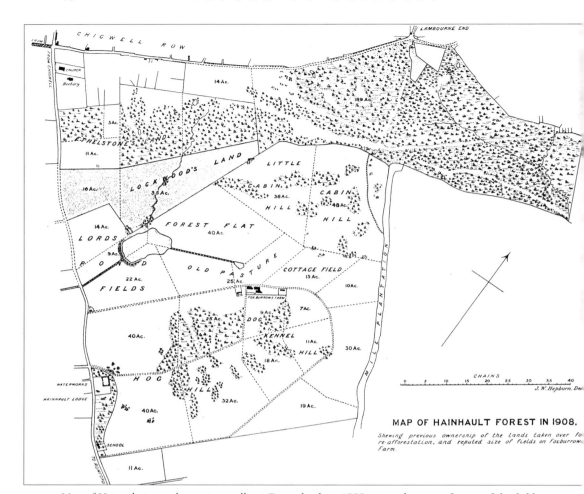

Map of Hainault (note alternative spelling) Forest lands in 1908 giving the sizes of some of the fields.

The enterprising F. Cole's refreshment rooms. This establishment provided accommodation and refreshment for the numerous groups of cyclists who visited the Fairlop area in the early part of the twentieth century. The reference to 'Ye old Fairlop Oak', on the central advertisement on the upper floor, refers to the Fairlop Fairs, suppressed in the nineteenth century.

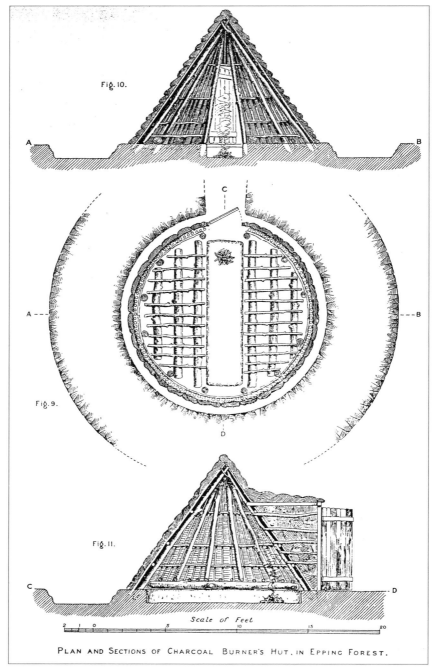

Fig. 10.

Fig. 9.

Fig. 11.

Scale of Feet

PLAN AND SECTIONS OF CHARCOAL BURNER'S HUT, IN EPPING FOREST.

Plan and sections of the charcoal burner's hut. In 1909 the *Essex Naturalist* recorded the brief revival of this old trade in Epping Forest during September/October 1908 by two Loughton men. In February 1909 two other men also revived the practice; they were from Collier Row on the edge of Hainault Forest which had been associated with charcoal burning from medieval times. Thus for a short while S.H. Warrin was able to record the terminology, processes and even the construction of the charcoal burner's hut which was based on excavated examples from the days of prehistoric man (*Essex Naturalist*, volume XVI, p. 65).

WOODFORD GREEN & WOODFORD BRIDGE

Woodford Bridge, 1904. A community grew up here around the original ford over the Roding which gives Woodford its name. Most of Woodford's medieval tenants lived here, according to a list made in about 1235. Several of these people actually took their names from a local feature, for example, Robert de Ponte, Alexander and Goscelin atte Bridge and William ad Acquam.

A country prospect on the road between Barkingside and Woodford, 1929.

Some of the houses at the Boys' Garden City, 1916. This was a development built by Dr Barnardo at Woodford Bridge.

Woodford Bridge, 1924. New housing and improved transport links brought about gradual changes. The area became less attractive and less rural.

A view over the water to the clubhouse at Woodford Green, 1929. In 1876 Woodford was still made up of scattered hamlets. The best shops were situated by the green at Woodford Green, alongside some sizeable mansions.

Looking for tiddlers – girls on a trip out to Woodford Bridge, 1929.

A view round the bend, Woodford Bridge Road, 1929.

The dining hall at Bancrofts School, Woodford Wells, 1908. This hamlet took its name from a medicinal spring first mentioned in 1285 and described in 1766 as being near the Three Wells public house.

An open-air service at Woodford Bridge, 1928. This was held by members of Ilford High Road Baptist Church.

Reflections in the water at Woodford Green, 1929. Woodford Green and the Woodford Wells were connected by a line of compact roadside cottages. Each of the three outlying hamlets of Woodford had its own church. The spire of Woodford Green church can be seen projecting above the trees. Three of Woodford's famous sons were Sydney Smith (1771–?), the humorous poet; Coventry Patmore (1823–?), author of *The Angel in the House* and other poetry; G.E. Street (1824–1881), the eminent Victorian architect.

Florida Cottages, Woodford, 1908.

THE CHIGWELL FRINGE

A sketch of the Old King's Head, Chigwell, 1906. Coller in his History of Essex *comments 'Chigwell is generally regarded as one of the sweetest villages in the County. It abounds in beautiful woodland scenery, extending in several parts along the verge of the forest.' Dickens wrote much of* Barnaby Rudge *at the King's Head. As he had said to his friend Forster, 'Chigwell, my dear fellow, is the greatest place in the world.' It is thought that Dickens combined the features of two inns to create 'The Maypole' in* Barnaby Rudge *– 'The King's Head' at Chigwell and also the old 'Maypole' at Chigwell Row, which is marked on Morant's map in the* History of Essex. *This inn later became a private house and a new, less-picturesque 'Maypole' was built in front on part of the old village green.*

The atmosphere in the Old Chest Room, the Old King's Head, was reminiscent of Charles Dickens and the days of horse carriages.

Hainault Road, Chigwell.

Hainault Road, Chigwell, 1930. The name Chigwell was first recorded in the Domesday Book and it almost certainly dates back to the days of pagan worship of holy wells. The original meaning of 'Chigwell' was 'The spring of Cicca's people'.

The Woodlands, Chigwell Row. Huntsmen and dogs hold the field. Dickens viewed this spectacle a hundred years before on his visits to the area.

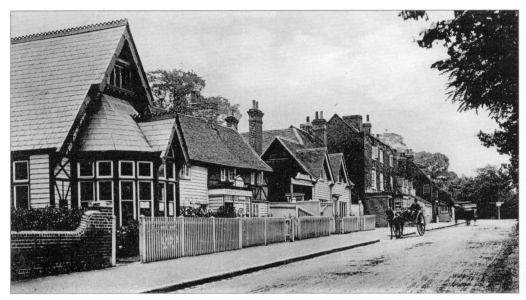

Chigwell Street, 1906.

Bishops Hall, Lambourne, 1905. This was the home of Colonel Lockwood, MP for the Epping or Western Division of Essex. The hall may have been named after the family of Roger Byssop who gave land to the prior of Dunmow in about 1273.

Hainault Forest, Chigwell Row.

116263.

Hainault Forest, seen from Chigwell Row. George Shillibeer, who brought the first bus to London, lived at The Grove, Chigwell Row, which accounted for the name Shillibeer Lane which was given to a road that ran alongside the grounds. It is believed that the model for Gainsborough's picture *The Woodcutter* was a local woodsman. Hainault Forest, Chigwell Row was also the camping ground of many gypsies until the London County Council took over the forest. They were ejected from the woods and went to settle at Eastwood, near Southend, although some remained nearby. In 1887 Chigwell Row was described as 'a neat village and parish formed out of Chigwell in 1867 in which year its church (All Saints), a stone building in the early decorated style, was built. The village enjoys a fine view and there are round it many good residencies of London merchants and others.'

View from the church tower, Chigwell Row. A description of Chigwell Row in 1908 said it 'was constituted an ecclesiastical parish, December 10, 1867, and is about 2 miles east of Chigwell of which civil parish it forms a portion, 4 miles east from Woodford station and 3½ miles from Buckhurst Hill . . . both on the Great Eastern Railway. . . . A station for this parish, called Grange Hill was opened in 1903 on the new loop line of the Great Eastern Railway from Ilford to Woodford. The church of All Saints consecrated in 1867, is a building of stone, in the style of the Transition from the Early English to Decorated, and consists of a lofty clerestoried nave, aisles, western porch and a tower, added in 1903. A parish room was built in 1854, and the old National School enlarged in 1889, and now called 'All Saints Schoolroom' is also used for parochial purposes.' Several persons in Chigwell Row are listed as providers of refreshment in 1908. They were obviously catering to the weekend and year-round holiday visits of Londoners to the area which includes Hainault Forest. Chigwell Row is a high point from which views can be obtained over the Thames to the Kent hills. Below it is Hainault Forest, once the hunting preserve of kings and court. Now over 1,000 acres of delightful fields and woodland are open to the public for recreation.

A MOVING STORY

Outside Ilford station, 1909. This bustling view would have been the first thing those considering moving to Ilford would have seen. The number of shops would probably be a surprise to some, who might have imagined that Ilford was 'in the sticks'. House agents, coal-order offices (coal was then the main fuel for heating), furniture stores, linen and curtain shops — everything was available close to the centre and, if the proposed home was on the outskirts where the countryside still held sway, then it could be delivered. Trams would whisk you to anywhere between Ilford and Chadwell Heath or Ilford and Barkingside. The electricity department of Ilford fought hand to hand with the gas company to supply your power needs. The General Bus Company were about to link the Ilford suburbs into their new Londonwide network. The railway not only had Ilford, Seven Kings and Goodmayes stations open on the main line but their new loop line connected Ilford with Newbury Park, Barkingside and Fairlop. The tale of the first four decades of the twentieth century as far as Ilford was concerned was truly a moving story.

Tramcar No. 7 crossing Ilford station bridge, 1906. As the new tramway service developed, improvements such as covers for the top deck and the ordering of more luxurious cars were implemented.

General Bus Company vehicle in Cranbrook Road in the 1920s. Here, close to the station were many house agents. The building on the right, occupying a prominent corner site, has had various uses and still remains today.

Looking south from Gants Hill roundabout, 1960s. This area has seen an increase in housing and office developments.

The Newbury Park station was transformed from a country stop in to a futuristic interchange between rail and road. This took place just after the Second World War when the Central underground line took over the old Great Eastern Railway north of this point. This severed the direct rail link with Ilford and made a connection to Gants Hill, a new station in a tunnel, and also to Leytonstone and Stratford to the west and south-west.

Looking back again to the early days of Ilford's 'moving story' and the tram terminus at Barkingside with the tram men and locals in delightfully relaxed mode, c. 1906. To the right of the tram is the former police station building which changed its use as the village developed. It had first been a private house, then it became a vicarage in about 1851, surprisingly becoming the Mossford Arms beerhouse by 1860. A large modern police station now stands on the site. George Tasker, in *Ilford Past and Present* (1901),

predicted the changes which took place at Barkingside, 'Barkingside has great possibilities before it. At present its population is mainly rural, but with the opening of the loop line of railway between Ilford and Woodford, via Barkingside and with the completion of the electric tram system from Ilford, the place is sure to develop rapidly and what is now land on which wheat, oats and vegetables grow so readily will ere long be covered by houses . . .'

TYPES OF HOUSES ON GRANGE HILL ESTATE

A postcard advertising the types of houses on the Grange Hill Estate in the 1930s. Development had reached as far as Chigwell Row. It had taken a considerable time for estate building to reach this point. Note the mock 'Tudorbethan' facings on the modern houses – reminiscent of the simpler life which had been destroyed by development.

The Great Eastern Railway's Grange Hill station, 1916. Open since 1903 on the loop line from Ilford, this stop still mainly served the needs of visitors to the countryside, but development would soon begin in this area, as can be seen from the advertisement opposite. Meanwhile the lanes around the station were attractive to cyclists and ramblers at weekends and holiday times.

A mass exodus of Sunday school children on Ilford station platform, 1912. They were probably going on a daytrip to Southend – one wonders if any children were left in the town. The numbers emphasize how many new residents, particularly younger couples, had come to live in the town. The population of the town grew sensationally from 10,913 in 1891 to 78,188 in 1911. The main developer at this time was A. Cameron Corbett. He operated on a grand scale with local contractor Robert Stroud, and he ensured all his estates had good access to a railway station. He worked with the railway to enable new stations to be built at Seven Kings and Goodmayes and to encourage the very necessary reconstruction of Ilford station itself. The story of the local line in the first four decades of the twentieth century was one of steady expansion as the number of tracks and stations increased. At first the line was under the jurisdiction of the Great Eastern Railway and then, after 1924, the London and North Eastern Railway. After the Second World War British Railways electrified much of the line.

Children by the embankment at Fairlop station, which can be seen in the background. They are on a ramble with their parents and have probably just finished their picnic before boarding the steam train back to civilization. In the 1920s Fairlop still consisted of fields and farms. There are still considerable acres of open land, which are now used as sports grounds. Large areas, however, have been covered by housing and by industrial and commercial developments.

Rural bliss on a smallholding north of Ilford, 1910. A small plot and a basic cottage could still enable people to enjoy a life of semi self-sufficiency on a small income.

CHARMING FREEHOLD HOMES
in a DELIGHTFUL District and a most
choice and exclusive position on . . .

MONKHAM'S ESTATE, WOODFORD GREEN

NO LEGAL COSTS   NO ROAD CHARGES—CONCRETE ROADS
Footpaths Edged with Shrubs.

PRICES, FREEHOLD - From £1,195

COMPRISING: Drawing Room 16' x 13'. Dining Room 18' x 12'.
Kitchen 13' x 9'. Front Bedroom 16' 9" x 13'. Back Bedroom
16' 6" x 13'. Third Bedroom 10' 6" x 8'. Bathroom, with
Coloured Tiling 8' x 8'. Garage, Brick built. Hall and
Ground Floor in oak, and every modern accommodation.
Each house built 25 ft. from back of footpath.

Whole of the Estate laid out under Town Planning Scheme in
Ideal Surroundings, near to Epping Forest, part adjoining the
new Knighton Wood ⟩ ⟩ ⟩ Few minutes from Woodford Station
(L.N.E.R.) and several 'Bus Routes to City and West End.

SALWAY HILL ESTATES
Monkham's Drive, Woodford Green
'Phone: BUCKHURST 0519

An advertisement for the Monkham's Estate, Woodford Green, 1935. With the surge of housebuilding in the mid-1930s, after the war and the depression, the 'big sell' entered the housing market. Advertisements like this were to be found not only in newspapers but in sizeable brochures offering houses in all the new suburbs around London, together with snippets of household and historical information.

FAIRLOP STATION

AERODROME BUILDINGS

AERODR

LNER loop line conne
with NEW ILFORD TUI
brings FAIRLOP to
12 Miles from BANK

On 7 April 1938 the press had details of a proposed new London Airport at Fairlop. If the scheme had developed no one would have ever heard of Heathrow. The impact on Ilford would have been dramatic and perhaps more of London's green belt would have been destroyed. The approach of the Second World War torpedoed the scheme. This aerial photograph, which appeared in the press of the time, points out

the advantages of the proposed tube link, an extension of the Central Line. This development was delayed by the advent of the Second World War and was not completed until the late 1940s.

An aerial view of Ilford, 1930. This area was one of the greatest concentrations of suburban development around London. The *Victoria County History* comments, 'During the rapid expansion in the late nineteenth and early twentieth century the type of residential development in Ilford was remarkably uniform. The link between development and the opening of railway stations suggests that most of the new inhabitants went daily to London.' As we have seen this type of resident was specifically encouraged by the methods of developers such as Cameron Corbett who mainly relied on ground rents for his profit, selling the houses at little more than cost and making access to already good transport even better. There is no doubt that Ilford owes its successful development to its proximity to London, its opportune independence from Barking and its promotion of civic leaders capable of capitalizing on Ilford's natural advantages.